LEON

Sweet Treats

NATURALLY FAST RECIPES

LEON

NATURALLY FAST RECIPES

Sweet Treats

By Henry Dimbleby, Kay Plunkett-Hogge, Claire Ptak & John Vincent

PHOTOGRAPHY BY GEORGIA GLYNN SMITH · DESIGN BY ANITA MANGAN

conran
OCTOPUS

Contents

Introduction 7

Cakes & bakes 8

Pies & tarts 18

Chocolate treats 28

Frozen desserts 36

Fruity puddings 44

Conversion chart 60

Index 62

Introduction

We started Leon because we believed that fast food could also be good food. We wanted our dishes to taste amazing. We wanted a trip to Leon to bring with it all of the excitement we remembered from visiting the fast food joints of our childhood, but we wanted people to feel great afterwards – not sluggish and guilty.

In short, we believed that you should be able to have your cake and eat it. This book is intended to help you do just that. It is a selection of puddings and other goodies, all made from natural ingredients.

Some are luxurious, indulgent (the Warm Gooey Chocolate Cakes spring to mind – see page 34) and perfect for a party or a private treat. Others are designed for people who are trying to cut out sugar, wheat or dairy – or who simply want to make their pleasures a bit less sinful. There's a flourless Clementine Polenta Cake (see page 10) and a sugar-free chocolate cake (see page 13) that is useful for children's parties: you should find your tiny guests don't flip out quite as much as usual.

We've got a versatile Upside-down Apple and Cardamom Tart (see page 27) – just don't try cooking it on the barbecue, as Henry once did – and, in the frozen section, the only ice cream recipe you'll ever need (see page 40). Use it as your base for every ice cream, and add whatever flavours you like, from Baileys to caramelized breadcrumbs. There's also a recipe for Raw Chocolate Banana Torte (see page 38), for those of you who are on a serious health kick.

Whatever the situation, we hope this book will provide the solution when you are looking for that sweet fix.

Happy cooking.

Henry & John

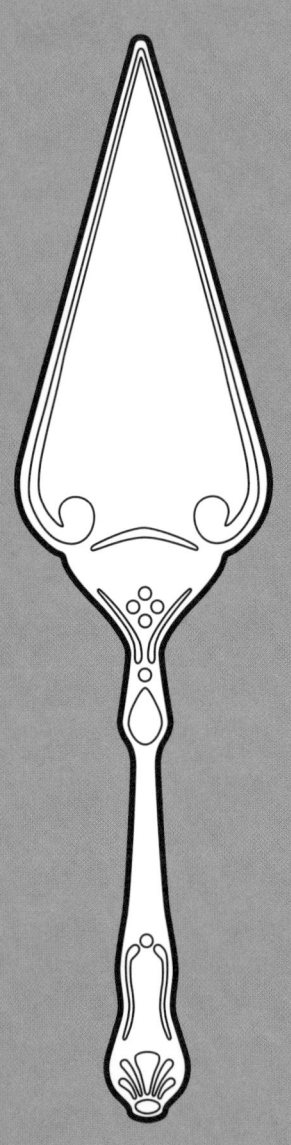

CAKES & BAKES

Clementine Polenta Cake

SERVES 12 • PREPARATION TIME: 25 MINUTES • COOKING TIME: 50 MINUTES • WF GF

This moist flourless cake is perfect for teatime, but also makes a beautiful pudding when drizzled with a little cream or topped with a blob of yoghurt.

For the cake:
250g **unsalted butter**, very soft
250g **caster sugar**
2 **free-range eggs**
200g **fine polenta**
100g **ground almonds**
1 teaspoon **baking powder**

grated zest and juice of
   3 **clementines**
2 tablespoons **lemon juice**

For the syrup:
50ml **runny honey**
juice of 1 **clementine** and
   1 **lemon**

1. Heat the oven to 170°C/340°F/gas mark 3½. Butter a 25cm round cake tin and line it with baking paper.

2. In a large mixing bowl, beat the soft butter and sugar until very pale in colour and fluffy. Add the eggs one at a time, beating well after each addition.

3. In a separate bowl, whisk together by hand the polenta, ground almonds and baking powder. Add to the butter mixture and beat well. Fold in the clementine zest and juice and lemon juice before scraping the mixture into your prepared tin.

4. Bake in the oven for 50 minutes, or until a skewer inserted into the centre of the cake comes out clean.

5. To make the syrup, heat the honey with the clementine and lemon juice in a small pan over a gentle heat until runny, then pour over the cake whilst its still hot. Leave to cool in the tin.

TIPS

* Wonderful served with Greek yoghurt or double cream.

* You can experiment with other kinds of citrus in this recipe. It works very well with lemon.

* You can use agave nectar instead of honey for the syrup (this would go nicely with lime juice in place of the clementines).

A Good Chocolate Cake

SERVES 8 · PREPARATION TIME: 30 MINUTES · COOKING TIME: 35 MINUTES
COOLING AND DECORATING TIME: 2 HOURS · ♥ ✓ DF V

A great cake for a children's party if you don't want your house terrorized by children high on sugar and food colouring. It is vegan, but they'll never know it.

For the cake
150ml **hot water**
80g **cocoa powder**
200ml **agave nectar**
200ml **coconut milk**
juice of ½ a **lemon**
80ml **sunflower oil**
2 teaspoons **vanilla extract**
180g **white spelt flour** or
   plain flour
½ teaspoon **baking powder**
1½ teaspoons **bicarbonate**
   of soda
a pinch of **salt**

For the icing
50g **coconut oil**
200g **dark chocolate**
1 teaspoon **vanilla extract**
50ml **agave nectar**

flowers from the garden,
   to decorate (optional)

TIPS

* Instead of flowers,
you could add some
raspberries to the cake
and arrange a few on
top for decoration.

1. Heat the oven to 160°C/325°F/gas mark 3. Grease and line a 20–23cm cake tin with baking paper.

2. Whisk together the hot water and cocoa powder until smooth. Add the remaining wet ingredients and set aside.

3. In a large bowl, sift together the flour, baking powder, bicarbonate of soda and salt. Pour the wet mixture over the dry and whisk in a circular motion from the centre of the bowl, moving outwards to combine. Pour the mixture into the cake tin.

4. Bake in the oven for about 35 minutes, or until a skewer inserted comes out clean and the cake is springy to the touch. Let it cool for 10 minutes before turning it out on to a wire rack to cool completely.

5. For the icing, put all the ingredients into a heatproof bowl and place over a pan of barely simmering water to melt, and stir. Move the cake to a serving plate and drizzle the chocolate icing over it.

Glasgow Banana Bread

SERVES 4–6 • PREPARATION TIME: 15 MINUTES • COOKING TIME: 30 MINUTES • V

A wholesome fruity loaf.

2 **smallish eggs** (or 1 large)
125g melted **unsalted butter**
2–3 tablespoons **whole milk**,
   or more if needed
4 **very ripe bananas**
280g plain **spelt flour**
1 teaspoon **bicarbonate of soda**
2 tablespoons **wheatgerm**
   (optional)

90g **molasses** or **muscovado
   sugar**
100g **cashew nuts**
90g **poppy seeds**
grated zest of 1 **lemon**
a pinch of **salt**

1. Heat the oven to 180°C/350°F/gas mark 4, and grease and line a 2lb (900g) loaf tin.

2. Whisk together the eggs, melted butter and milk. Mash up the bananas roughly and add to the mixture.

3. In a separate bowl, sift together the spelt flour and bicarbonate of soda. Stir in the wheatgerm (if using), sugar, cashew nuts, poppy seeds, lemon zest and salt.

4. Gently fold the egg mixture into the dry ingredients – do not over-stir.

5. The mix should be a good dropping consistency – firm enough to stick to a spoon, but able to drop off if you turn it upside down. Add a little more flour or milk to get the correct consistency.

6. Put the banana bread into the greased tin and bake for about 30 minutes, or until a knife comes out cleanly.

TIPS

* If you would like the bread to have a Polish feel, add more poppy seeds.

* You can also add dates, prunes or raisins, or some grated carrot, to diversify the banana flavour.

* Serve it in slices, spread with butter.

Pam Edwards's Date & Walnut Loaf

MAKES: 8–10 SLICES • PREPARATION TIME: 15 MINUTES • COOKING TIME: 30 MINUTES • V

Glenn Edwards says: 'Mum used to bake this loaf for the holidays in the family caravan. Whilst Mum reckons it's best the next day, Dad always preferred it buttered, still warm from the oven (in fact, I'm not sure it ever lasted until the next day?).'

225g **self-raising flour**
1 level teaspoon **salt**
1 level teaspoon **bicarbonate of soda**
250ml **milk**

85g **pitted dates**
55g **sultanas**
55g **walnut halves**
2 tablespoons **golden syrup**
85g **demerara sugar**

1. Heat the oven to 190°C/375°F/gas mark 5. Grease and line a 20 x 10cm loaf tin.

2. Sift the flour, salt and bicarbonate of soda into a bowl. Put the remaining ingredients into a food processor and blend for about 20–30 seconds. Stir into the dried ingredients and, when they're well combined, pour the mixture into the prepared loaf tin.

3. Bake in the oven for 30 minutes, then leave to cool on a wire rack.

4. This loaf is at its best served the next day, sliced and buttered … if it lasts that long.

TIPS

* Glenn is a rather new member of the Leon team. He's very tall. You may find him at one of our shops dressed as a chef. Or 'test-eating'. Pam is his mum. Back in the 70s, she was a beauty queen. We think this cake's a beauty, too.

PAM AND GLENN, CUMBRIA, 1980

Susanna Mattana's Amaretti Macaroons

MAKES: 24 • PREPARATION TIME: 20 MINUTES PLUS COOLING
COOKING TIME: ABOUT 40 MINUTES • WF GF V

Our friend Susanna can really cook. This macaroon recipe has been handed down to her from her grandma via her mother. No saint's day, wedding or feast in her native Sardinia would be complete without these glorious almond clouds …

500g **ground almonds**
300g **caster sugar**
grated zest of 1 **lemon**
6 **egg whites**
24 **whole blanched almonds**

1. Heat the oven to 170°C/325°F/gas mark 3½. Line a large baking sheet with baking parchment.

2. In a large bowl, thoroughly mix the ground almonds, sugar and lemon zest using your hands.

3. In a separate bowl, beat the egg whites into stiff peaks – really give them a good seeing to! Then gently fold them into the almond mixture, a spoonful at a time, mixing carefully but thoroughly.

4. Now form them into 24 'meatballs' (as Susanna says). Place them on the baking sheet, push a blanched almond gently into the top of each one and pop them into the oven for about 40 minutes. They should be golden brown and smell gorgeous. Cool before serving.

Susanna Mattana and Massimo Usai run a wonderful, warm Sardinian restaurant in Putney, southwest London, called Isola del Sole. Their handmade pastas are to die for. Susanna's pumpkin or artichoke raviolis are sigh-inducing, like angels' pillows.

Massimo supports Arsenal.

PIES & TARTS

Leon Pecan Pie

SERVES 8–10 • PREPARATION TIME: 50 MINUTES, PLUS CHILLING
COOKING TIME: 1 HOUR 10 MINUTES • WF GF V

A simple, rich, gluten-free pecan tart that has become a classic in the restaurants. Baked by Craig Barton, one of our favourite bakers.

For the sweet pastry:
150g **butter**
100g **caster sugar**
1 **free-range egg**, plus 1 **yolk**
270g **gluten-free plain flour**

For the filling:
50g **butter**
225g **golden syrup**
2 tablespoons **caster sugar**
1 teaspoon **cornflour**
2 large **free-range eggs**
200g **pecan nut halves**

1. Cream together the butter and sugar with a wooden spoon or in a free-standing electric mixer until smooth.

2. Add the egg and egg yolk and mix until fully incorporated. Add the flour and quickly bring it together in a ball. Wrap the pastry in clingfilm and refrigerate for at least 30 minutes.

3. Butter a 23–25cm fluted flan tin. Roll the pastry out on a floured surface to about 3–5mm thick and line your tart case with it. Trim the edges and chill in the fridge for 30 minutes. Meanwhile, heat the oven to 160°C/325°F/gas mark 3.

4. Line the chilled pastry case with baking paper, and fill it with baking beans to stop it shrinking while it's being baked. Bake in the oven for 20 minutes then remove the baking beans. Return to the oven and bake for a further 5 minutes. The pastry should be a nice blonde colour. Set aside to cool.

5. Put the butter and golden syrup into a medium saucepan over a low heat. When it becomes runny, take it off the heat and whisk in the sugar.

6. In a small bowl, whisk the cornflour and eggs until smooth then add to the saucepan.

7. Fill the baked pastry with the pecan halves. Pour the golden syrup mixture on top and fill it up to just below the edge of the case. Put into the oven, taking great care not to spill any liquid over the sides, as this might make it difficult to remove it from the tin once it's baked.

8. Bake for about 40 minutes, or until the tart is a dark golden in colour and has slightly risen in the middle. Take out of the oven and leave to cool in the tin.

TIPS

* Serve cold for tea, or warm with vanilla ice cream.

Pecan Pie

Momma's Apple Pie

SERVES 6 • PREPARATION TIME: 20 MINUTES, PLUS CHILLING • COOKING TIME: I HOUR • V

'As American as Mom and Apple Pie,' as the saying goes … Serve this double-crust, rather old-fashioned pie with cream, if you like. But to be really authentic, you should really have it à la mode with a scoop of excellent vanilla ice cream. God Bless America.

500g **plain flour**
250g **unsalted butter**, straight
   from the fridge
a large pinch of **sea salt**
2 tablespoons **caster sugar**,
   plus an extra tablespoon
   for the top
1 small glass of **iced water**
1 **egg**, beaten, to glaze

For the filling:
900g **apples**, peeled, cored and
   sliced – we use a mixture of
   Braeburn, Bramley and Cox's
100g **caster sugar**
the juice of 1 **lemon**
½ teaspoon **ground cinnamon**
a good grating of **nutmeg**

1. First make your pastry: Measure out the flour into a large bowl. Cut the cold butter into small pieces and drop them into the flour. Coat them with flour, then start rubbing the flour and butter together with your fingertips, lifting it and gently working it until you have what looks like fine breadcrumbs.

2. Add the salt. Then the sugar. Mix well. Now add the iced water a teaspoonful at a time, working everything together with your hands until the pastry just comes together. Don't add too much water, or you'll get a hard pastry. Roll it into 2 loose balls, cover with clingfilm and refrigerate for at least 30 minutes.

3. Heat the oven to 180°C/350°F/gas mark 4 and grease a 23cm pie dish with butter.

4. Put the sliced apples into a large bowl. Sprinkle over the sugar, lemon juice, cinnamon and nutmeg and mix well.

5. Take the pastry balls out of the fridge and roll them out, one at a time, into circles the size of your pie dish. Line the bottom of the dish with one circle. Tip in the filling, then cover with the other circle and crimp the bottom and top together.

6. Bake the pie in the oven for 20 minutes. Then remove it from the oven and brush the top with the beaten egg. Sprinkle over the extra caster sugar and bake for another 40–50 minutes, or until golden brown and cooked through. Serve with vanilla ice cream.

Marshmallow-topped Sweet Potato Pie

SERVES 6–8 • PREPARATION TIME: 35 MINUTES • COOKING TIME: 50 MINUTES • V

This recipe comes from our friend Andi Oliver.

1 x 375g (approx.) pack of
   sweet shortcrust pastry
4 **pink-fleshed sweet potatoes**
6 large spoons of **honey**, or
   agave nectar or any **sweetener**
   that you prefer
1 teaspoon **ground nutmeg**
1 teaspoon **ground cinnamon**

1 teaspoon **ground allspice**
1 teaspoon **vanilla extract**
2 tablespoons **desiccated coconut**
   (optional)
3 **free-range egg whites**
1 packet of **white mini**
   marshmallows

1. Heat the oven to 180°C/350°F/gas mark 4.

2. Roll out the pastry with a rolling pin big enough to line a fluted flan tin measuring about 25–28cm. Bake blind (as in step 4 on page 20) for around 25 minutes, until the pastry is golden. Remove from the oven and set aside to cool, leaving the oven on.

3. Peel the sweet potatoes and cut them into cubes. Boil until soft, then mash them well.

4. Put the sweet potatoes into a large bowl with the honey, nutmeg, cinnamon, allspice, vanilla extract and the coconut (if using). Mix thoroughly.

5. Beat the egg whites well in a separate bowl, then add to the sweet potatoes and whisk the mixture together for a few minutes. Pour the mixture into the pastry case and bake in the already warm oven for around 20 minutes.

6. When the top of the pie has a few browned peaks it is ready to come out of the oven. Gently arrange the marshmallows on top in any design that you like.

7. When you are ready to eat the pie, place it under a hot grill to toast the marshmallows, which will go golden and start to melt very quickly. Keep a close eye on it so that they don't burn.

Hattie's Blackcurrant Tart Canelle

SERVES 6–8 • PREPARATION TIME: 25 MINUTES, PLUS CHILLING • COOKING TIME: 30–35 MINUTES • V

Serve this beautiful tart cool with vanilla ice cream or crème fraîche.

170g **plain flour**
85g **unsalted butter**
85g **caster sugar**
2 **free-range egg yolks**
1 tablespoon **water**
1 level tablespoon **ground cinnamon**

225g **blackcurrants**, off the stalk
extra **caster sugar** to add to the currants, plus more to sprinkle over
milk or **beaten egg**, to glaze

1. Heat the oven to 180°C/350°F/gas mark 4.

2. To make the pastry in a food processor, put in the flour, butter, sugar, egg yolks, water and cinnamon and blitz until it comes together into a ball. Remove from the machine, cover with clingfilm and chill well for at least an hour in the fridge.

3. To make the pastry by hand, mix together the flour, butter, sugar and cinnamon with your fingers until you have a breadcrumb-like consistency. Slowly add the egg yolks and water until the mixture comes together into a ball. Cover with clingfilm and chill well.

4. Put the blackcurrants into a pan, cover generously with caster sugar, and put over a low heat. Stir regularly, and when you are sure that all the sugar has melted, turn up the heat until the fruit is bubbling and thick-looking. Remove from the heat.

5. Roll out the pastry 1cm thick and line an 18cm fluted flan tin, gathering up any trimmings. Fill the flan case with the blackcurrant compote, and roll out the trimmings to make a thin and neat extra strip to go around the edge. There should be enough pastry left to make a lattice pattern over the top of the tart if you wish.

6. Brush the pastry with milk or beaten egg, and bake in the oven for 20–25 minutes, until the pastry is golden. Let cool, sprinkle with caster sugar and serve.

Upside-down Apple & Cardamom Tart

SERVES 4 • PREPARATION TIME: 10 MINUTES • COOKING TIME: 30 MINUTES • V

The flavour of the cardamom transforms this simple apple tart.

3 **cardamom pods**	40g **butter**
juice of 1 **orange**	4 **apples** (about 650g)
4 tablespoons **soft brown sugar**	200g **puff pastry**

1. Heat the oven to 180°C/350°F/gas mark 4.

2. Crush the cardamom pods and keep the little seeds. In a saucepan, heat the orange juice, sugar, butter and cardamom seeds until thick and bubbly. Pour the syrup into a 25cm flan tin (obviously it cannot be one with a push-out bottom or the syrup will seep through and go everywhere).

3. Quarter the apples and cut out the cores. Cut each quarter into thin slices and arrange symmetrically on top of the syrup in the flan tin.

4. Roll out your pastry and lay it over the top of the apples in the tin. Cut off the excess around the edges and crimp to seal. Sprinkle a little more sugar on top if you like.

5. Place the tin in the oven for 30 minutes, or until the pastry has risen and is golden. Put a serving plate on top, hold it tightly and flip the whole thing over. Tap the bottom of the tin to ensure that all the apple slices are on the plate, and remove it. A magically neat and tidy tart will appear.

TIPS

* Serve with cream or Quick Custard (see page 47).

* This is one of those versatile recipes. You can use almost any fruit – pears, plums, apricots, nectarines, peaches and oranges all work well. You can also play with the syrup: try a red wine syrup with star anise and plums. White wine, vanilla and nectarine make a subtle combination; with oranges, try using shortcrust pastry and a really treacly syrup made with a little molasses as well as sugar.

* When using soft fruit in this tart it is better if the fruit is slightly under-ripe.

CHOCOLATE TREATS

Leon Chocolate Mousse

SERVES 4 • PREPARATION TIME: 25 MINUTES • COOKING TIME: NONE • ✓ WF GF V

This is a recipe from the first cookbook (one of the magnificent creations of Leon co-founder Allegra McEvedy). We included it here because it is a classic Leon treat and we know there are lots of people who want to make it for themselves.

100g **dark chocolate** (70% cocoa solids)
30g **unsalted butter**
2 **free-range egg yolks**
1 shot of **dark espresso**
a drop of **orange oil** or very finely grated zest of ½ **orange** (optional)
3 **free-range egg whites**
15g **fructose**

1. Melt the chocolate and butter until smooth in a large, heat-proof bowl in the microwave, or over a pan of simmering water, making sure the water does not touch the surface of the bowl.

2. Separately whisk the egg yolks until nearly white and thick in consistency. Gently stir the whisked yolks into the butter and chocolate, then stir in the coffee and the orangey bit, if you are adding it.

3. Use an electric hand whisk to whip the egg whites to soft peaks, then add the fructose and whisk for another minute just to get that shine.

4. Beat a third of the egg white into the chocolate mixture until smooth, then add the next third more gently, and the last with the strokes of an angel.

5. Neither over-mix nor leave white streaks, then divide the mousse into pretty things and leave in the fridge for an hour.

TIPS

* You can use Cointreau or Grand Marnier instead of orange oil or zest. Or you can leave out the orange flavour altogether.

* If you don't have fructose, you can use 20g of caster sugar (you need more because fructose is slightly sweeter).

Sweet Popcorn with Chocolate Drizzle

SERVES 4 • PREPARATION TIME: 20 MINUTES • COOKING TIME: 10 MINUTES • ♥ ✓ WF GF V

A rainy Sunday afternoon snack that's almost as much fun to make as it is to eat.
Make it alongside a salty popcorn and settle down on the sofa with a good movie.

2 tablespoons **vegetable oil**
100g **popcorn**
100g **dark chocolate**, broken into pieces
75g **salted butter**
50g **golden syrup**

1. In a large saucepan with a tight-fitting lid, warm the oil over a medium heat. Pour the popcorn into the saucepan and cover it with the lid. The corn will begin to pop quite quickly. When the popping slows down, by which time most of the kernels should have popped, remove the pan from the heat and open the lid to release the steam. Set aside.

2. Melt the chocolate in a small heatproof bowl over a pan of barely simmering water, making sure the water does not touch the surface of the bowl. Stir occasionally. Meanwhile, line a baking sheet with baking paper.

3. Melt the butter and golden syrup together in another saucepan, stirring continuously.

4. Fold the popped corn into the butter and syrup mixture and stir well to coat. Spread the popcorn out to cool on the baking sheet.

5. When the chocolate has melted, drizzle it over the sweet popcorn.

TIPS

* Leave out the golden syrup if you want something less sugary.

Claire's Chocolate Hazelnut Power Pills

MAKES: 12 BALLS OR 24 POWER 'PILLS' • PREPARATION TIME: 15 MINUTES
COOKING TIME: NONE • ♥ ✓ WF GF DF V

These pocketable snacks taste sensational and give you a powerful burst of energy.
Make a massive batch and give some to your friends.

125g **raw hazelnut butter**
100g **Brazil nuts**, finely chopped
50g **dried cherries**, preferably
   without oil or sweetener added,
   finely chopped
2 tablespoons **shelled hemp seeds**
1 tablespoon **chia seeds**, ground
   in a mortar
3 teaspoons **cacao nibs**, chopped
2 teaspoons **raw cacao powder**

3 teaspoons **raw honey**
1 teaspoon **maca root powder**
1 teaspoon **coconut oil**
½ teaspoon **blue green algae**,
   spirulina, or **other source**
   of chlorophyll
seeds from ¼ of a **vanilla pod**
extra **cacao powder**, **hemp seeds**,
   chia seeds or **coconut shreds**,
   to coat

1. Mix all the ingredients together in a bowl (easiest done using your hands).

2. Shape the paste into small balls or pills and gently roll them in
   the extra cacao powder, hemp seeds, chia seeds, coconut shreds,
   or a combination of any of these.

3. Chill for 15 minutes. Keep refrigerated.

The Americas are a very fertile land, and the ancient civilizations that lived
there knew of the many health properties of the roots, fruits, seeds and herbs
that grew there. Some of these plants – like chia seeds and maca root – are being
rediscovered, and many of them are becoming widely available.
Be brave and experiment with them. The flavours and
textures are fascinating.

CLAIRE

Warm Gooey Chocolate Cakes

SERVES 6–8 • PREPARATION TIME: 10 MINUTES • COOKING TIME: 7 MINUTES • WF GF V

One of those chocolate-oozing-out-of-the-middle puddings that is not nearly as hard to make as your awestruck guests will assume.

1 tablespoon **caster sugar**
85g **unsalted butter**
150g **dark chocolate**
a pinch of **salt**
5 tablespoons **cocoa powder**
100g **free-range egg whites** (about 2)
icing sugar, to dust

1. Heat the oven to 200°C/400°F/gas mark 6.

2. Butter individual mini pie dishes and sprinkle each one with some caster sugar.

3. Melt the butter, chocolate and salt in a large, heat-proof bowl over simmering water. When all is melted, sift in the cocoa powder.

4. In a separate bowl, whisk together the egg whites and sugar until soft peaks form. Combine with the melted chocolate by folding gently and trying not to knock out too much air.

5. Spoon the mixture into the moulds and bake in the oven for just 7 minutes. Serve immediately or let cool and dust with icing sugar before serving.

TIPS

* Whatever you do, do not over-bake these. They continue to bake slightly as they cool down, so take them out of the oven just before you think they are ready.

* Serve with pouring cream and a splash of Cognac if you have some around.

* You could also make a whipped Chantilly cream by adding a small amount of sugar and vanilla extract to whipping cream.

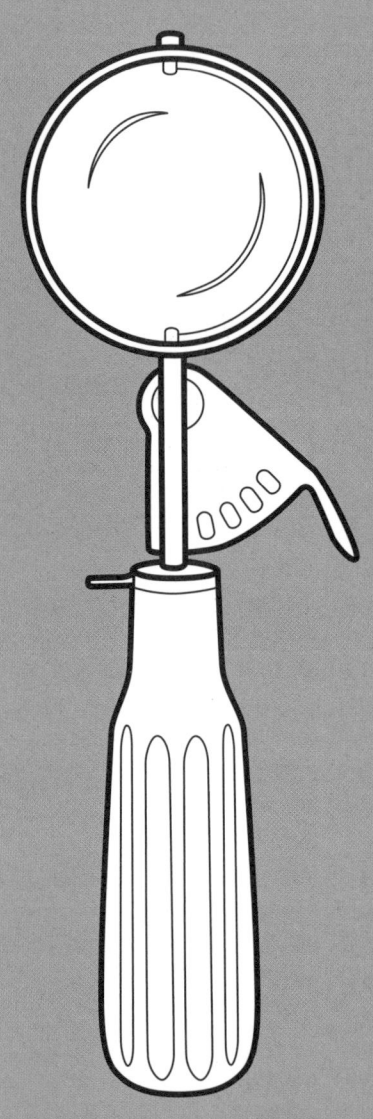

FROZEN DESSERTS

Raw Chocolate Banana Torte

SERVES 10 • PREPARATION TIME: 20 MINUTES • COOKING TIME: NONE • ♥ ✓ WF GF DF V

It is important to start by making the base layer so that it has time to set in the freezer.

100g **whole almonds**
6 **pitted dates**
50g **sunflower seeds**
a pinch of **salt**
60ml melted **coconut oil**
4 **bananas**

2 **avocados**
2 tablespoons **tahini**
6 tablespoons **cacao powder**
½ teaspoon **vanilla powder**
2–4 teaspoons **honey**, depending
  on how sweet you like it

1. Combine the almonds, dates, sunflower seeds and salt in a food processor. Melt the coconut oil in a bain-marie to avoid overheating. Once the oil has liquefied, pour it into the food processor while the engine is running. The mixture should end up as more or less one uniform ball.

2. Divide into 2 parts, one larger (about ¾), one smaller (about ¼), and put the smaller one aside. Press the larger part into a 20cm loose-bottomed cake tin with the base of your palm until it is about 5mm thick. Put it into the freezer to set while you prepare the other layers.

3. Peel the bananas, mash up 2 and cut the remaining 2 into even slices.

4. Peel the avocados and discard the stone. Place the flesh in a food processor with the tahini and blend well. Add the cacao and vanilla powder, then the honey. At the very end, dilute ever so slightly with a little water.

5. Remove the bottom layer of the torte from the freezer and cover it with the mashed bananas. At this point, roll out the second, smaller chunk of base layer dough until it is about as thick as a pancake and gently place on top of the mashed bananas.

6. Gently arrange the sliced bananas over the entire surface.

7. Cover with the avocado layer and place in the fridge until you are ready to serve it.

Nanabhai's Kulfi

FROM AYAZ HOSSAIN

MAKES 18–20 SMALL KULFI MOULDS • PREPARATION TIME: 10 MINUTES
COOKING TIME: 20 MINUTES • WF V

Ayaz says: 'On family holidays to India, my grandfather (or as we say, Nanabhai) used to attempt to cheer us up with his creation of 'ice cream'. It would take him the best part of the day, stirring away in the heat of Kolkata. I have now eaten kulfi at various restaurants but none bring back those memories quite like the recipe below.'

a good pinch of **saffron**
1 litre **whole milk**
2 tablespoons **cornflour**
1 x 397g tin of **sweetened
    condensed milk**

6 **whole green cardamom pods**,
    finely powdered or the
    seeds, ground
25g **almonds** or **pistachios**, soaked
    overnight, peeled and sliced

1. Soak the saffron in a tablespoon of the whole milk and set aside.

2. In a separate small bowl, make a paste with the cornflour and 2 tablespoons of the whole milk.

3. Mix the rest of the milk and the condensed milk together in a pan and bring to the boil, stirring continuously. Reduce the heat and simmer for 10 minutes, stirring all the time.

4. Add the cornflour paste to the pan and continue stirring until the mixture thickens.

5. Remove from the heat, but keep stirring and allow to cool slightly.

6. Add the saffron in its milk and mix well. When completely cool, add the powdered cardamom and almonds or pistachios. Pour into kulfi moulds and freeze.

TIPS

* Ayaz uses his grandfather's stainless steel kulfi moulds. If you don't have any, you can use paper cups, half-filled, or small yoghurt pots.

* To speed up the process, you can cool the mixture quickly by placing the pan into a large bowl of cold water.

Ice Cream Base

MAKES 900ML · PREPARATION TIME: 30 MINUTES · FREEZING TIME: UP TO 5 HOURS · WF GF V

The base for almost all ice creams. Once you have mastered this, you can experiment by adding fruit purées, dried fruits, booze, candied nuts, or even caramelized days-old breadcrumbs. This base is made with both double cream and whole milk, making it a little lighter than usual and consequently a better vehicle for other flavours.

5 **free-range egg yolks**
300ml **double cream**
300ml **whole milk**
180g **caster sugar**

1. Make sure the eggs are at room temperature. Crack them into a large bowl and whisk them briefly to break up the yolks.

2. Pour the cream into a plastic container that will hold all the ingredients and also fit into your fridge. Place a fine sieve over this and then set aside.

3. Put the milk and caster sugar into a small pan. Bring to just under the boil, stirring to make sure the sugar dissolves.

4. Pour the hot milk slowly into the eggs, whisking as you go.

5. Pour the milk-and-egg mixture back into the pan and place back on the hob. Stir constantly with a wooden spoon or a heatproof plastic spatula. The custard is ready when you can swipe a finger through the custard and leave a trail on the back of a spoon. This should happen quite quickly.

6. Immediately pour the custard through the fine sieve into the reserved cream. Sieving removes any bits of cooked egg, and if you are flavouring the custard with vanilla or coffee beans, for example, they will be strained out here.

7. Give the ice cream base a good stir and taste. If it needs a pinch of salt or a teaspoon of vanilla extract or brandy, now is a good time to add it.

8. Chill the base until cold (it's a good idea to start the day before you're ready to freeze it, or early in the morning). Pour into an ice cream machine and freeze, according to the manufacturer's instructions.

TIPS

* When tasting your ice cream base, bear in mind that it will taste sweeter at room temperature than when it is frozen.

* It is easy to flavour your ice cream base with vanilla pods or cinnamon sticks. Any of your favourite spices can make a delicious ice cream. Steep them like tea in with the milk in step 3 (opposite), then strain. Here are a few guidelines:
  • For Coffee Ice Cream: 50g of freshly roasted whole coffee beans.
  • For Vanilla Ice Cream: 1 vanilla pod, split, seeds scraped out.
  • For Cinnamon Ice Cream: 1 short stick of soft Ceylon cinnamon.
  • For Cardamom Ice Cream: 3 whole cardamom pods.

Raspberry Ripple Ice Cream

MAKES 1.1 LITRES • PREPARATION TIME: 30 MINUTES • FREEZING TIME: UP TO 5 HOURS • WF GF V

Leave out the vodka if you are making this for children, but it really lifts the flavour of the raspberries (and the spirits).

> 1 x quantity **vanilla Ice Cream Base** (see page 40)
> 200g **raspberries**
> 4 tablespoons **icing sugar**
> 2 tablespoons **vodka**
> 2 teaspoons **vanilla extract**

1. Make the vanilla ice cream base.

2. Put the raspberries, icing sugar, vodka and vanilla extract into a blender or food processor and blitz to a thick purée. Push through a sieve to remove the seeds.

3. Before the ice cream is fully frozen (but when it's pretty stiff), stir in the raspberries in thick seams. Continue to freeze in the freezer (see below) or in your ice cream machine.

FREEZING ICE CREAM

The classic method that uses egg yolk to make a custard base results in dense, luxurious ice cream. But you cannot simply leave it in a freezer, otherwise long, crunchy ice crystals will form. This is where an ice cream machine comes in useful. Otherwise, you'll need to freeze the mixture in a shallow, wide container, that will fit into your freezer. Every 30 minutes use a whisk to stir and break up the ice that has formed until it becomes a light ice cream.

Saffron & Orange Blossom Ice Cream

SERVES 4 • PREPARATION TIME: 10 MINUTES, PLUS STANDING • FREEZING TIME: UP TO 5 HOURS
COOKING TIME: 15 MINUTES • ✓ WF GF V

This really is sunshine-chilled-on-a-plate – one of our favourite summer creations.
Serve with a slab of the Clementine Polenta Cake on page 10, and with a hunk of
honeycomb sliding down the side …

1 teaspoon **orange flower water**
a large pinch of **saffron**
285ml **milk**
4 **egg yolks**
4 tablespoons good **runny honey**
285ml **double cream**

1. Infuse the orange flower water with the saffron and set aside.

2. Bring the milk up to the boil but DO NOT let it boil. Take it off the
   heat, add the pinch of saffron and orange flower water, and set aside
   for 30 minutes.

3. In a large bowl, beat the egg yolks with the honey until combined
   and creamy. Add the milk mixture to the egg yolks and stir.

4. Pour the mixture back into the pan and heat gently, stirring.
   Again, DO NOT let it boil. When it coats the back of your spoon
   remove from the heat. Leave to cool.

5. When it's cold, stir in the double cream. Pour into your ice cream
   maker, and churn as per its instructions.

FRUITY PUDDINGS

Baked Apples

SERVES 4 • PREPARATION TIME: 15 MINUTES • COOKING TIME: APPROX 1 HOUR
♥ ✓ DF V (WF GF IF YOU USE GLUTEN-FREE BREAD)

Baked apples are easy and perfect for a chilly autumn night. They deserve to be more fashionable than they are.

4 medium **apples**, such as Cox's or Braeburn
1 slice of stale **bread**, white or gluten-free
150g homemade or other good-quality **mincemeat**
a pinch of **sea salt**

1. Heat the oven to 180°C/350°F/gas mark 4. Line a baking tray with baking paper.

2. Dig out the cores of the apples without going all the way through to the bottom, then place them on individual squares of kitchen foil, big enough to wrap the apples, on the paper-lined baking tray.

3. Tear the bread into pea-sized pieces and mix with the mincemeat and salt. Pack the bread mixture into the apples. Bring the foil up and wrap it loosely around them, then bake in the oven for 45 minutes to an hour, until tender.

TIPS

* Serve with Quick Custard (see opposite) or double cream.

* Instead of mincemeat, the following work well as toppings:
  • Raspberries, brown sugar and breadcrumbs, served with vanilla ice cream.
  • Apricots, sultanas and sour cherries, plumped in red wine and sugar, drizzled with butter and served with double cream.

Roasted Peaches

SERVES 4 • PREPARATION TIME: 5 MINUTES • COOKING TIME: 15 MINUTES
WF GF (DF V IF NOT USING CREAM)

Sometimes the best things are the simplest. Make sure you get the best peaches you can afford.

4 ripe **white or yellow peaches**
8 tablespoons **white wine**
100g **caster sugar**
double cream, to serve

1. Heat the oven to 180°C/350°F/gas mark 4.

2. Halve the peaches and remove the stones. Arrange the peach halves in a roasting tin, cut side up. Add the white wine and sprinkle over the caster sugar.

3. Bake in the oven for 12–15 minutes, until the fruit is bubbly and a little golden on the edges. Serve with the cream.

TIPS

* When the peaches come out of the oven, they will bubble as they start to cool down. Arrange them on small plates and pass the jug of cream.

* Use ripe delicious peaches. If they are underripe, no amount of cooking will be able to save them.

Jossy's Jewelled Rhubarb & Mango

SERVES 4 • PREPARATION TIME: 20 MINUTES • COOKING TIME: I HOUR • ♥ WF GF DF V

This is a simple but sublime combination, which also looks beautiful. The appearance of the deep yellow mango with the clear pink rhubarb, and the combination of their contrasting flavours, is wonderful.

500g **early forced thin-stalked champagne rhubarb**
1.5cm piece of **fresh ginger**
2 or 3 **star anise**
150ml **cranberry juice**

juice of 2 **limes**
50g **caster sugar**
1 large or 2 small ripe **mangoes**
a few **mint leaves**, to decorate

1. Heat the oven to 170°C/340°F/gas mark 3½.

2. Slice the rhubarb across on the diagonal into 5cm pieces. Peel the ginger, cut it in half and slice into small, very thin pieces.

3. Arrange the rhubarb, ginger and star anise in a wide ovenproof flan dish. Put the cranberry juice, lime juice and sugar into a saucepan and bring to the boil, stirring until the sugar has dissolved. Boil fiercely for 2 minutes, then pour on to the rhubarb.

4. Cover the dish tightly with foil and put it on the centre shelf of the oven for about 1 hour, until the rhubarb is very soft. Remove from the oven, take off the foil and leave to get cold.

5. Cut open the mangoes and cut the flesh off the stone, then skin them and slice into thin strips. Arrange the mango strips among the rhubarb, with the star anise dotted on top, then chill in the fridge. Before serving, decorate with mint leaves.

Blueberry Cheesecake

SERVES 8-10 • PREPARATION TIME: 20 MINUTES • COOKING TIME: 45 MINUTES-1 HOUR • V

A rich, creamy cheesecake cut by a sharper fruit topping. Luxurious.

125g **digestive biscuits**
125g **gingernuts**
90g **unsalted butter**
550g **cream cheese**
125g **caster sugar**
2 teaspoons **lemon juice**
seeds from 1 **vanilla pod**
200g **crème fraîche** or **soured cream**
100g **thick Greek yoghurt**
3 large **free-range eggs**

TIPS

* Cherries are always welcome on a cheesecake, as are cranberries. Add a teaspoon of almond extract for the cherry version, and finely grated orange zest for the cranberry version.

For the blueberry topping:
2 small punnets of **blueberries**
2 teaspoons **cornflour**
3 tablespoons **water**

1. Heat the oven to 160°C/325°F/gas mark 3.

2. Crush the biscuits to a fine powder in a food processor. Decant them into a bowl. Melt the butter and pour it over the biscuit crumbs, stirring to fully coat them.

3. Press the biscuit mixture into the base of a deep 20cm springform or loose-bottomed cake tin, then put it into the fridge to firm up.

4. Beat the cream cheese, caster sugar, lemon juice and vanilla seeds together until creamy. Mix in the crème fraîche and yoghurt, then the eggs and beat until smooth.

5. Spoon the filling over the chilled biscuit base. Smooth over the top and bake in the oven for 45 minutes, or until the filling has set (it may need a further 10 minutes).

6. Place the tin on a wire rack to cool completely, then run a small paring knife around the inside of the tin to help release the cheesecake from the tin.

7. Toss the blueberries in the cornflour and put them in a small saucepan with the water. Heat whilst stirring until the blueberries are bubbling and start to break up. Allow to cool then spoon over the top of the cheesecake.

Roasted Figs with Triple Sec

SERVES 4 • PREPARATION TIME: 10 MINUTES • COOKING TIME: 15–20 MINUTES
(BUT DO CHECK ON THEM, AS SOME FIGS COLLAPSE MORE QUICKLY) • WF V

Simple roasted figs, with a splash of liqueur.

8–12 ripe **black figs**
25g **butter**
the grated zest of ½ an **orange**

4 tablespoons **triple sec**
2 tablespoons **honey**
a pinch of **salt**

1. Heat the oven to 180°C/350°F/gas mark 4.

2. With a sharp knife, make a cross in the pointy end of each fig, cutting them about halfway through. Then squeeze the fat bottoms gently so that each fig opens up like a flower. Lay the figs in a roasting tray or ovenproof dish, and dot each one with a little butter.

3. Mix the orange zest and liqueur together in a bowl, and pour evenly over the figs. Drizzle over the honey and season with a pinch of salt. Pop them into the oven for 15–20 minutes. Serve hot, with some of the sauce spooned over them and some good ice cream or yoghurt.

TIPS

* Triple Sec is made from orange peel, and crops up most frequently in cocktails. If you don't want to use the alcohol, replace it with orange juice and serve the figs accompanied by some good vanilla ice cream.

Bo-That's Bananas

SERVES 4–6 • PREPARATION TIME: 10 MINUTES • COOKING TIME: 8–10 MINUTES • ♥ ✓ WF GF DF V

This is a simple version of a Thai dish called *gluay buat chee*, which means 'bananas that have been ordained as nuns'. We guess it's because they are clothed in white milk, the same colour as the robes of Thai Buddhist nuns. It's really delicious, and very simple to make. This version is named after Kay's elephant Bo-That, because he *loves* bananas.

4–6 **bananas**
200ml **coconut milk**
a 5cm piece of **pandan (screwpine) leaf or a drop of pandan essence**
2 tablespoons **palm sugar**
a large pinch of **salt**
150ml **coconut cream**

1. Peel the bananas and slice them in half lengthways, then chop them into 3 so that each banana gives you 6 pieces.

2. Heat the coconut milk with the pandan leaf and, when it comes to the boil, add the banana pieces, sugar and salt. Bring back to the boil and add the coconut cream.

3. Gently bring back to a simmer and let cook for 3–4 minutes. Remove the pandan leaf and serve warm or at room temperature.

TIPS

* Kay eats this dish for breakfast, hot on a cold morning or chilled on a hot morning.

* You can find pandan leaves or pandan essence in most Asian stores. If you can't find them, don't worry. It's just as good without them.

Spelt Pancakes

MAKES: APPROX. 20 PANCAKES • PREPARATION TIME: I HOUR 10 MINUTES
COOKING TIME: I HOUR • ♥ ✓ V

The key is to throw the pancakes as high as you can without getting them stuck to the ceiling.

100g **plain spelt flour**
a pinch of **salt**
1 **free-range egg**
200ml **whole milk**

50ml **ale** or **lager**
butter, for the pan
lemon juice and **caster sugar**,
  to serve

1. Measure the flour into a large bowl and add the salt.

2. Whisk in the egg from the centre of the bowl, moving outwards in a clockwise motion.

3. Add the milk and whisk to a smooth batter.

4. Strain the batter into a measuring jug and stir in the beer. Chill the pancake batter for at least an hour.

5. Heat a non-stick frying pan or iron crêpe pan until hot, then add a little butter. Stir the batter a little before pouring a small amount into the pan. Swirl the batter quickly around the pan to coat in a thin, even layer.

6. Cook for a minute or so, until it starts to bubble, then slide a thin spatula beneath the pancake to loosen it and flip it over. Flip 'em high – that is the fun bit. Cook for another minute or so before piling the pancakes up on a plate to cool.

7. To serve, squeeze lemon juice over the pancakes, sprinkle with sugar, then fold into triangles or roll into scrolls.

TIPS

* Allowing the batter to rest makes all the difference. Don't be tempted to skip that step.

* You can use agave nectar instead of caster sugar. You can also substitute white flour for the spelt flour if you want to. And of course you can use water instead of beer.

Apricot & Cherry Galette

SERVES 6–8 • PREPARATION TIME: 30 MINUTES • COOKING TIME: 45–50 MINUTES • V

This is a free-form, open-face tart and it can be used for all different kinds of fruit.

For the pastry:
125g **plain flour**, plus extra for dusting
a pinch of **salt**
a pinch of **sugar**
85g cold **unsalted butter**, cut into 1.5cm pieces
4 tablespoons **ice-cold water**

For the galette:
2 tablespoons **sugar**
1 tablespoon **plain flour**
1 tablespoon **ground almonds** (optional)
225g **cherries**, washed and halved, stones removed
450g fresh **apricots**, washed and halved, stones removed
1 **free-range egg**, beaten

1. Combine the flour, salt and sugar in a bowl and either cut in the cold butter with the back of a fork or use two knives.

2. Avoid over-mixing – leaving larger chunks of butter than you would expect will make the pastry more flaky. Drizzle in the water and bring it all together into a ball without working the dough. Wrap in clingfilm, then flatten into a disc and let it rest in the fridge for about 45 minutes.

3. Heat the oven to 200°C/400°F/gas mark 6 and line a baking sheet with baking paper. Allow the pastry to come to room temperature so its easier to work.

4. Dust a work surface with flour and roll out the dough into a circle about the size of a dinner plate. Put it on the baking sheet and return it to the fridge for a few minutes.

5. Remove the pastry circle from the fridge and sprinkle the sugar, flour and ground almonds over, leaving a 5cm border around the outside.

6. Arrange the fruit on top of the almonds – you can put the cherries in the middle and the apricots in circles around them, or make up your own pattern.

7. Fold over the pastry rim to create a crust. Brush the rim with beaten egg, and bake in the bottom half of the oven for 45–50 minutes, until the fruit is squashy.

8. When cooked, transfer the galette on to a wire rack to cool.

9. Serve warm or cold, with vanilla ice cream or whipped cream. Or simply enjoy it on its own with a cup of tea.

CONVERSION CHART FOR COMMON MEASURES

LIQUIDS

15 ml	$^1/_2$ fl oz
25 ml	1 fl oz
50 ml	2 fl oz
75 ml	3 fl oz
100 ml	3 $^1/_2$ fl oz
125 ml	4 fl oz
150 ml	$^1/_4$ pint
175 ml	6 fl oz
200 ml	7 fl oz
250 ml	8 fl oz
275 ml	9 fl oz
300 ml	$^1/_2$ pint
325 ml	11 fl oz
350 ml	12 fl oz
375 ml	13 fl oz
400 ml	14 fl oz
450 ml	$^3/_4$ pint
475 ml	16 fl oz
500 ml	17 fl oz
575 ml	18 fl oz
600 ml	1 pint
750 ml	1 $^1/_4$ pints
900 ml	1 $^1/_2$ pints
1 litre	1 $^3/_4$ pints
1.2 litres	2 pints
1.5 litres	2 $^1/_2$ pints
1.8 litres	3 pints
2 litres	3 $^1/_2$ pints
2.5 litres	4 pints
3.6 litres	6 pints

WEIGHTS

5 g	$^1/_4$ oz
15 g	$^1/_2$ oz
20 g	$^3/_4$ oz
25 g	1 oz
50 g	2 oz
75 g	3 oz
125 g	4 oz
150 g	5 oz
175 g	6 oz
200 g	7 oz
250 g	8 oz
275 g	9 oz
300 g	10 oz
325 g	11 oz
375 g	12 oz
400 g	13 oz
425 g	14 oz
475 g	15 oz
500 g	1 lb
625 g	1 $^1/_4$ lb
750 g	1 $^1/_2$ lb
875 g	1 $^3/_4$ lb
1 kg	2 lb
1.25 kg	2 $^1/_2$ lb
1.5 kg	3 lb
1.75 kg	3 $^1/_2$ lb
2 kg	4 lb

OVEN TEMPERATURES

110°C......(225°F).......Gas Mark ¹/₄
120°C......(250°F).......Gas Mark ¹/₂
140°C......(275°F).......Gas Mark 1
150°C......(300°F).......Gas Mark 2
160°C......(325°F).......Gas Mark 3
180°C......(350°F).......Gas Mark 4
190°C......(375°F).......Gas Mark 5
200°C......(400°F).......Gas Mark 6
220°C......(425°F).......Gas Mark 7
230°C......(450°F).......Gas Mark 8

Working with different types of oven

All the recipes in this book have been tested in an oven without a fan. If you are using a fan-assisted oven, lower the temperature given in the recipe by 20°C. Modern fan-assisted ovens are very efficient at circulating heat evenly around the oven, so there's also no need to worry about positioning.

Regardless of what type of oven you use you will find that it has its idiosyncrasies, so don't stick slavishly to any baking recipes. Make sure you understand how your oven behaves and adjust accordingly.

MEASUREMENTS

5 mm .... ¹/₄ inch
1 cm .... ¹/₂ inch
1.5 cm .... ³/₄ inch
2.5 cm .... 1 inch
5 cm .... 2 inches
7 cm .... 3 inches
10 cm .... 4 inches
12 cm .... 5 inches
15 cm .... 6 inches
18 cm .... 7 inches
20 cm .... 8 inches
23 cm .... 9 inches
25 cm .... 10 inches
28 cm .... 11 inches
30 cm .... 12 inches
33 cm .... 13 inches

KEY TO SYMBOLS / NUTRITIONAL INFO

♥   LOW SATURATED FATS

✓   LOW GLYCAEMIC (GI) LOAD

WF   WHEAT FREE

GF   GLUTEN FREE

DF   DAIRY FREE

V   VEGETARIAN

TIPS   COOKING TIPS, EXTRA INFORMATION AND ALTERNATIVE IDEAS.

Index

A

almonds, ground
    amaretti macaroons 16–17
    apricot & cherry galette 58
    clementine polenta cake 10
amaretti macaroons 16–17
apple
    baked 46
    & cranberry crumble 48
    Momma's apple pie 22–3
    upside-down apple & cardamon
      tart 26–7
apricots
    & cherry galette 58–9
    upside-down tart 27
avocados, raw chocolate banana torte 38

B

bananas
    Bo-That's 55
    bread 14
    raw chocolate banana torte 38
Barton, Craig 20
blackcurrants, Hattie's tart canelle ... 25
blueberry cheesecake 52–3

C

cake
    blueberry cheesecake 52–3
    chocolate 12–13, 34–5
    clementine polenta 10–11
cardamom 27, 39, 41
cheesecake, blueberry 52–3
cherry
    & apricot galette 58–9
    cheesecake 52
chocolate
    cake 12–13
    drizzle for popcorn 32

hazelnut power pills 33
    mousse 30–1
    raw chocolate banana torte 38
    warm gooey cakes 34–5
cinnamon ice cream 41
clementine polenta cake 10–11
coffee
    chocolate mousse 30
    ice cream 41
conversion chart 60–1
cranberry
    & apple crumble 48–9
    cheesecake 52
cream, Chantilly 34
cream cheese, blueberry cheesecake 52
crumble, cranberry & apple 48
custard, quick 47

D

dates
    Glasgow banana bread 14
    raw chocolate banana torte 38
    & walnut loaf 15
dried fruit
    in banana bread 14
    chocolate hazelnut power pills ... 33
    date & walnut loaf 15

E

Edwards, Pam, date & walnut loaf 15
eggs
    chocolate mousse 30
    quick custard 47

F

figs, roasted, with Triple Sec 54

G

galette, apricot & cherry 58–9
Glasgow banana bread 14

H

hazelnut & chocolate power pills 33
Hossain, Ayaz 39

I

ice cream
    base 40–1
    Nanabhai's kulfi 39
    raspberry ripple 42
    saffron & orange blossom 43

K

kulfi, Nanabhai's 39

M

macaroons, amaretti 16–17
mango & rhubarb, jewelled 51
marshmallows, sweet potato pie 24
Mattana, Susanna 16
McEvedy, Allegra 30
mincemeat, in baked apples 46
mousse, chocolate 30–1

N

Nanabhai's kulfi 39
nectarines, upside-down tart 27
nuts
    chocolate hazelnut power pills ... 33
    date & walnut loaf 15
    pecan pie 20–1
    see also almonds, ground

O

Oliver, Andi 24
oranges, upside-down tart 27
oven temperatures 61

P

pancakes, spelt 56–7

pastry
    puff 27
    shortcrust 22
    sweet 20, 24, 25
peaches
    roasted 50
    upside-down tart 27
pears, upside-down tart 27
pecan pie 20–1
pies 20–4
plums, upside-down tart 27
polenta & clementine cake 10–11
popcorn with chocolate drizzle 32

R

raspberry ripple ice cream 42
rhubarb & mango, jewelled 51

S

spelt
    chocolate cake 13
    pancakes 56–7
sweet potato pie,
    marshmallow-topped 24
symbols, key to 61

T

tarts 24–7

W

walnuts, & date loaf 15

An Hachette UK Company
www.hachette.co.uk

First published in Great Britain in 2015
by Conran Octopus Limited, a part of
Octopus Publishing Group, Carmelite House,
50 Victoria Embankment, London EC4Y 0DZ
www.octopusbooks.co.uk

This book includes a selection of previously
published recipes taken from the following
titles: *Leon Naturally Fast Food*, *Leon Baking &
Puddings* and *Leon Family & Friends*.

A CIP catalogue record for this book is
available from the British Library.

Publisher: Alison Starling
Managing Editor: Sybella Stephens
Assistant Editor: Meri Pentikäinen
Art Director: Jonathan Christie
Art Direction, Design and Illustrations:
    Anita Mangan
Design Assistant: Abigail Read
Photography: Georgia Glynn Smith
Production Controller: Allison Gonsalves

ISBN 978 1 84091 705 5

Printed and bound in China

10 9 8 7 6 5 4 3 2 1

A note from the authors …
Medium eggs should be used unless
otherwise stated.

We have endeavoured to be as accurate as
possible in all the preparation and cooking
times listed in the recipes in this book.
However, they are an estimate based on our
own timings during recipe testing, and should
be taken as a guide only, not as the literal
truth. We have also tried to source all our
food facts carefully, but we are not scientists.
So our food facts and nutrition advice are not
absolute. If you feel you require consultation
with a nutritionist, consult your GP for a
recommendation.

Also available in the Little Leon series …

Breakfast & Brunch • *Smoothies, Juices & Cocktails*
Soups, Salads & Snacks • *Brownies, Bars & Muffins*
Fast Suppers • *One Pot* • *Lunchbox*